STEEP STONY ROAD

STEEP STONY ROAD

by Daniel Picker

Viral Cat Press

Copyright © by Daniel Picker 2012

Published by Viral Cat Press
San Francisco, CA

All rights reserved. No part of this book may be reproduced in any form or by any means without the prior written consent of the publisher, excepting brief quotes used in reviews.

ISBN: 0615631673

ISBN-13: 978-0615631677

LCCN: 2012908922

Printed in the United States of America

For My Mother and Father

and My Family

CONTENTS

1. Sky Dark, Small Stars, 1
2. Poet's Cabin Door, 2
3. Old Bennington, Vermont, 3
4. On New Ceramic Vases, 4
5. The Wind Through The Window, 5
6. Beside The Field, 6
7. Great Blue Heron, 7
8. That Spring Day, 9
9. Evensong At Canterbury, 11
10. Sky Blue Eyes, 13
11. Art Supplies, 14
12. Geese, 15
13. The Cathedral Of Saint Francis Xavier, 16
14. Moss Hollow, 17
15. Sunday, 18
16. Summer Rain, 19
17. Connie Mack, 21
18. River Goddess, 22
19. Walden Pond, 23
20. Icarus Flies, 24
21. Orpheus, 25
22. Washington D.C., 26
23. Black Granite, 27
24. Green Mountain Boy – Quetzal, 29
25. Blackbird, 30
26. Monadnoc, 31
27. In Crows Woods, 33
28. America, 34
29. Of Those Heroic And His Shining Shield, 35
30. Ducks At Hopkins Pond, 37
31. Mountain Man, 38
32. Poppy's Walk, 39
33. With Poppy, 41
34. Sitting Beside, 42

35. Monticello, 43
36. Meeting Faith, 44
37. Friends Meeting, 45
38. Below The Buttonwoods, 46
39. Above a Station of the BART, 47
40. Words Of Cape Cod, 48
41. The Old School, 49
42. Summer Lush, 50
43. Wild Summer Swans At Coole, 52
44. To Thoor Ballylee, 53
45. At The Boathouse, 55
46. Through The Garden, 57
47. Bridges, 58
48. For Love Of The Modern, 59
49. Parker's Back, 61
50. Amistad's Dream, 62
51. At Eight, 63
52. Our Last Hike, 64
53. Last Late Night Song, 65
54. Field By The Corn, 66
55. Famine Vessel, 67
56. For My Father, 69
57. Gulls, 71
58. The Candle Burns, 72
59. Clothespin, 73
60. Those Days In Sun, 75
61. Soccer: Centennial Field, 77
62. Red Tail Hawk, 79
63. Headed Home, 80
64. Steep Stony Road, 81

ACKNOWLEDGEMENTS:

All of the poems in this book have appeared in print; some appeared in versions somewhat different from those that appear here. This book collects nearly all the published poems by Daniel Picker.

Acknowledgements are due to the editors of the following, in which these poems have appeared:

The Accelerated News of Chestnut Hill College, *Art Calendar Magazine* of Maryland, *Aurora: Stanford's Feminist Journal, Bridges, The Bucks County Writer, The Calliope Muse, Dial Tone: Stanford's Journal of the Arts, The Dudley Review* at Harvard University, *Elysian Fields Quarterly: The National Baseball Journal, Folio, The Haddonfield Monthly Meeting Newsletter, The Haddonfield Speaks Anthology, Intuitions: The National Humanities Journal for Teachers, The Marlboro Review* of Marlboro College, *May'ayan: The University of Pennsylvania's Jewish Literary Journal, Potash Hill, The Putney Post, Regio, RUNE: MIT Journal of Arts & Letters, Sequoia: The Stanford Literary Magazine, ShampooPoetry, Soundings East, The Thursday Review, The Tri-Lite, Vermont Literary Review, VT Folkus,* The poem "River Goddess" was chosen as the Winner of The Dudley Review Poetry Prize of Harvard University for 2010.

I would like to thank these editors, and the family, friends, and professors who have helped me over the years.

SKY DARK, SMALL STARS

Sky dark, small stars I only
wish the music to be there, rising
faint or bright above Orion

or singing here; Seven Sisters
not seen so bright, up this slope
the snow is crossed by light

tire tracks and worn by tree
shadows crossing at each
side. There is no breeze;

the snow squeaks beneath my
feet in this cold February night.

POET'S CABIN DOOR

I. With Franklin

I write by candlelight
slightly wavering as the dog
snores and the clock ticks
loudly; the gray icy snow
is quiet, and I have not
seen the stars tonight;
will they ever take
their proper places?

II. Poet's Cabin Door

The morning you came to breakfast
it was rainy, warm, mist
filled the trees nowhere near

as lovely as your hair.
But I can't be in
love with you,

and before we left,
the old worn white string
that passed through the heart

shaped door latch broke.

OLD BENNINGTON, VERMONT
For Robert Frost

Your legs grow tired as you walk
across that grass slope, of thick
laying down late summer grass.
The twilight breeze blows down
the dusk light, as the shadows grow,
below the rustling maples the wind
moves through over the spindly fence
posts. The orange light fades away
over those hills, as the lights of
the living light below. Here by these
old white clapboard houses are two who
never were much agreed. "I had a lover's
quarrel with the world"; those words
he hoped would never die: "Together
wing to wing, and oar to oar."

ON NEW CERAMIC VASES

For whoever may see those urns, and vases
in that case, they are yours, fine turquoise
shapes, once the artist's, now the viewer's

to peruse. With thin dark lines, like your
lashes, and the color of your eyes and brows.
She must have stood over those molds for hours

nurturing them. Pull those loaves from
the oven with the heat in your face;
witness the baked brown, with steam

rising warm. Now these shapes remind me
of everyone here. Years before I bent over
a polished copper plate etching, or clay

sculpting. There was honor present when the long
white–bearded sculptor wandered in, out, or
when the painter never said but a few words,

as he gleamed at my canvas: his chrysanthemums
in a bright window. I sweated that afternoon
and many more before. Those lines the color

of your eyes, never well enough known or
your countenance that hardly speaks, though
when you do, whispering, like those hand–turned

urns, once of cool wet earth, someday dust.

THE WIND THROUGH THE WINDOW

   Today is a spring morning, and the pale green maple flowers are blowing in a cool wind, as yellow–white sunlight falls between the tulip poplar and the oaks. Small violets are growing with deep shiny leaves, at the foot of the trunks, and daffodils are rising up, pale yellow with crisp, delicate green stems that are wet within. Below the rock garden, lush, deep onion grass grows, thick and heavy, like long maiden's hair. Out back in the yard, up in the maples, the black cat stalks blue jays with bright wings, through the gray limbs. The blue jays' wings are lit by the early rising of the spring sun. The cherry tree, overhanging the side porch of the house, is in pink and white blossoms which smell sweet, as the strong yellow forsythia and honeysuckle, by the side of the hedgerow.

   The limbs are touched by wind.

   In the kitchen, at the back of the house, with a porch and open screen door, above and before, a dozen white wooden steps going down to the cool earth, the cool wind comes up and in, over the cold white and turquoise tiles. As the sky brightens outside and the open windows begin to shine, letting in the warbling of birds' voices and the smells of spring flowers, the kitchen clock reads nine o'clock. A green radio plays and a brightly–decorated calendar is turned to April. The cabinets are turquoise, as is the stove. A strong–boned woman washes a white china cup in the warm faucet water rushing down over her hands. Her bleary morning eyes look out a side window. Her teenager is standing across the room, feeling the cold air, seeing the sunlight. She sings to herself in a low soft voice close to sobbing. Gospel music rises on the green plastic radio. It is Sunday.

   He speaks, "Mom, look at the sun through the trees; look at the wind move them; look at the light falling between them on the grass; look at the wind out there through the window."

   He walks over to her and touches her shoulder. She smiles a bit.

BESIDE THE FIELD

As a boy I walked down this road from school
or up, in the morning. Atlantic Avenue down
by the clattering tracks, by fields of thick onion
grass under the walnuts near crabapple. Those
bushes we played in as younger boys, and girls,
and hid by, near the great weeping willow
strong in any wind except that last late summer
storm that cracked that broad gnarled trunk in half.
Spring flowers, dandelions, then in the tufts
of seeds before they were yellow flowers, were
my friends with delicate green leaves.
I walked up that road every morning by white
cold dew glistening, and down every warm spring
afternoon with the robins and blue jays singing.

GREAT BLUE HERON

I see you majestic gray–blue atop
that fallen branch growing out
of this pond in the heart of town.
You move your long blue throat
and neck up, beak piercing to sky
but don't fly, content to stretch
then lift large feathered limbs,
wings only partially open, arms
with elbows, "prehistoric" a man
fishing half whispers. I half hope
to see you fly, just to witness
your great wings, your span's glory.
But worry: you're closer to
the opposite shore; could I make it
round to see you closer still? I
cross the wooden footbridge
then quietly scamper through woods
where I've seen ducks, geese,
five turtles on a fallen trunk
in the still pond water, but never
you. You turn to spy me out,
to look at me with your beady
black eyes, just as I ask where will
you fly? Just as you ask
silently of me with your lean
look, a short stare, "what
are you doing here?" I ask
the same of you in this old
town, an oasis of dark murk,
still water ancient with deep
psalms, and we both wonder
together leaning closer, your beak
toward me, is this our place too?
But then you quietly lift those
great blue wings and fly, just
one beat, one flap; this I longed

to see, you silently soar across
the pond, then to those other
trees, then lost to me left with
your great wings, beauty, regret.

THAT SPRING DAY
For Becky

In the winter we trekked across
the woods, the ash and maple
thick–trunked, gray like the sky

or ice as the sun began to fade
as our feet grew cold and wet.
Past the green conifers reaching

down with heavy snow–drooped
boughs; you said, "Hug a tree!"
smiling. We went to the gray house

with the siding worn, too,
and an old green pick–up rusting
as more warmth vanished when

no one was home. We trekked
back toward the burning orb,
and then too I knew what we held,

and how to hold it fading.
That last spring day after the orange
I handed you, then three winters

before, I was no longer lost in
the shining wheat of your long hair,
or the dancing coals of your eyes.

I know too the winter snow I've
grown to hold before you bent down
to the springing growth poking

through: keeping warm, a woman
is the orange behind the iron;
seen through blue eyes looking across

that field, after the simple rising
of your pennywhistle on that spring
day, I could hardly see you turn away.

EVENSONG AT CANTERBURY

The sky was dusk as we
left that English train,
panes that were lit by green
fields, lush full plains

tufted with July's
beauty as the sun lit
blue sky and you plunged
in George Eliot's

Middlemarch. But upon
that gray platform we two
ventured to cross town
for Canterbury Cathedral

for Evensong; there within
that grandeur I craned my
neck and eyes up the spire
to God's light beyond my sight.

And you the beauty leaned
like a willow in prayer
and song, here for another,
keeping your word. Unseen

promises He made, we made
to the spirit of the choir's
song, assembled in rows
beside the altar not far away.

I listened, prayed, sang
as best I could, thankful
one summer to be close
with you the beauty rang

there in Evensong in
Canterbury, just a day's
First–class train from Oxford
where we spent the term.

O, I prayed then you
could that season be mine,
beauty too fine to touch,
like a summer flower,

and now a decade after,
your beauty bright no doubt,
I remember far back
to that summer evening hour.

SKY BLUE EYES

We rode down the mountain that winter
to town where I bought a pair of boots,
then on the drive back up we stopped
at small shop for wine; we strolled the neat
wooden rows across nations of the globe
amazed by labels: bright green pastorals
of Switzerland where your grandmother
lived. I caught the light through clear glass
windows of west Brattleboro in your blue
glinting eyes, then we wound further back
up the mountain. Later that night we shared
those bottles, joked and laughed. After, I wrote:
"At night I dreamed of love on your face a gift."
Years later we met in Philadelphia
at summer and lounged on deep lush green grass
with sun and wind as you lay so close in
tight white slacks, then Chinese food, then to South
Street for dessert, a thick rich brownie we split,
"Like a newly–paved road!" you joked by
candlelight. Years from then you flew into
San Francisco; at night we first kissed below
grove of eucalyptus trees. Weeks later,
a night back in the city we closed a
Brazilian bar where you recalled Carnival
before we caught cab back to dark home
where glowing orange fire still burned
and slipped below cool fresh sheets and kissed
lips wet below full moon shadowed soft heft
before we slept. Late next morn we drove
in white Beetle with the top down across
the Golden Gate, beyond Sausalito
up the Sir Francis Drake, then stopped at shop
for cool drinks. Then climbing winding roads
through woods, then above cliffs, then with
winter wind blowing hair wild passed Muir
Beach, top down, the bright light on our
faces, and smiles – your blue eyes the sky.

ART SUPPLIES
> *In memory of Joseph M. Zinni*

I wish we were back
in that crowded art store
the shelves stacked
with linen pads, sable
brushes tiered like soft
beards of old masters,
and boxes of oil paints
arranged, their names
striking a song: cobalt
blue, cadmium yellow
alizarin crimson, deep
viridian green, all
boxed like shining friends
close and silver, ready
to ignite the world with
iridescence bright on bolts
of canvas and linen unfurled
and then you stretched
tight as the old masters would
who gathered light on their
brushes and smocks:
Rembrandt, Eakins, Van
Gogh, Monet, all waiting for
the moment the oils
blazed balanced in divine
harmonies eternal. So
neither of us is there;
I cannot hear the cutting
board blade descend
on mats and posters;
I cannot hear the Phillies
game on the radio
or the air conditioner
hum; I cannot see your
brown eyes and smile
except here: see, see.

GEESE

Before dusk I heard bagpipes sounding
over the summer air of these sloping Green Mountains
but couldn't find him, a brother, a friend
absent there. I searched through the dark green
boughs of conifers, past maple trunks in shadow.

And my step–brother, he too with the same name,
a few years older than I was then, when I heard
the geese sounding over the broad green Bucks County
plains, below the steep hard mountains lit by
failing light. Right below the stained bridge
we canoed, soaking each other with paddles,
splashing the murky water, deep brown, where fish

swim hidden, like souls or lights in eyes. We
laughed wildly that summer afternoon more than a decade
ago, beside trees waving, the towpath, green fields,
just below your hill, a hundred yards from the concrete
bridge, still with a chunk missing where you crashed.

THE CATHEDRAL OF SAINT FRANCIS XAVIER

They sat there, in that cathedral
with marble shining and rising like prayer
of saints now gone for centuries, held

reaching up for the heavens above:
tall pillars; beyond, white city light.
And what that Mass said to me of

Cana of Galilee, with rubble
and old earthen jars recalled,
dusty, broken beside straw, unchanged

for centuries, was love. The bride
had entered in soft white, behind a maid
dressed in the color of earth.

This Italian bridesmaid with the light
on her sunlit wheat hair. And those
to be wed sat in separate chairs

apart, a bride and groom as praises
swirled from far above us at a great
height where doves would light.

MOSS HOLLOW

That gray graveled muddy road I walked down
alone, and with a friend in early spring, and late
fall, that year before the last in Vermont, my
home. The earth was wet in spring, and in the late
summer evening, walks we kicked pebbles past
the gurgling gutter streams of the soft shoulders.
The earth was gray, as the March snow fields and sky,
and the iron, and ash, creosote of my stove, as we
walked beside the leach field opening up ahead,
on another grassier dirt road, wet wanting wear.
Under the springing leaves of the maples in dusk
light, and in the cooling late summer breeze of
early night, orange sunlight gone, every season
was so new there, by the rock walls above Moss Hollow.

SUNDAY

So no church this morning, just folding clothes,
mating socks, some old, others new. Cool
air whisks through my screen, a few squirrels scamper
below with a pale green prickly seed pod. The old fool
rises above the tops of waving cypress as the hamper
is emptied of the clean clothes, only to be those
closed up in drawers. O, to be as those who
doze still amid this louder clamor or as free
creatures speaking in tongues as they fly and swoop
down below this viridian towering pine tree.
Soon I will spread fresh sheets after pulling down

old pictures only put up to cover old holes.
In this bole below the pale blue heaven with
a few tiny tufts stretched I search for the cause
of all these strange voices, sounds of rustling boughs.
I look through the green to the bleached tan grass
beside the dusty ground of this California August.
I wonder what this day and evening may bring, lift
a song from these pages if words could speak soul's
wish. We will stand together above the umber cliffs,
and dream ahead over the broad Pacific, beside dust
where I have stood marveling at pelicans diving down.

SUMMER RAIN

Mid–summer when we were still
together drinking late at night in
those Cambridge cafes, dark small
stone steps, she close, tan before me,
or swatting tennis balls endlessly
back and forth, keeping the rally
going in humid late summer heat, my
chest glistening, or back in her room
sipping cold drinks, iced teas she
bought us, she in her red beach shorts.
Those nights the sun down, cool air across
the Charles and Mass. Ave., her
old shirts, worn smooth button–downs
open to night air, breeze, she beside me
still, here, now, only in these lines:
Guinness on tap in The Plough and Stars,
early evening before the Red Sox.
She with her ponytail and soft shining
eyes, still beside me at the bar –
then holding hands through the T
station through crowds underground
and outside Fenway then under
the bricks of that stadium.
Later that night back in Cambridge
walking her home back to that
brick river house, atop endless stairs
to those fourth floor dormered
windows, sitting beside her on her
bed, she kissing my neck.
She met me for the last afternoon
before John Harvard's statue, her red
wool baseball cap brim soaked, dripping,
her cotton jacket soaked through see–through,
pale creamy tan waves of wheat, her
lips tremulous, quiet trembling before

we embraced and kissed and walked
all over town again, over the old bricks,
through Cambridge Common past
some statue where we paused before walking
on together that summer, that rain.

CONNIE MACK

I would that we were back
there on that late Spring afternoon
sitting together in a row at Connie Mack
and we were still seven, and intact,
my whole family, not halved, or half
what it was and the lush green grass
opened up before us in sun, bill–
boards brilliant before us bright
white: M.A.B. Paints, Ballentine
Beer, Lucky Strike cigarettes:
"L.S.M.F.T." mom's brand,
all there: dad, mom, Robin,
Meg, Jeff, Dan, and Ned, and
Uncle Frank, and the Phillies in
white with simple red numbers
and lean, elegant, curving *P*
on their clean red caps, their flannels
as sharp as Uncle's light blue eyes,
as they warmed up tossing that white
cowhide ball, with red stitches,
or dug in the umber earth by
white lime lines, not black & white,
not the RCA TV at home, no here
in wooden, slatted, enameled
seats we all sat and smiled,
rubbed elbows, yelled, cheered
the Phillies: Johnny Callison,
Cookie Rojas, Chris Short,
Richie Allen there back then
under the balcony on the third
base side in heaven all seven.

RIVER GODDESS
   For W.E.B. Du Bois

Where the river is a strong brown–gold god–
dess and rushes beside a steep rocky bank,
here where a branch dips down cooling delicate
leaves, branches twiggy and leafy and the loud
current curves and courses over unseen rocks,
filling this ravine, chasm chamber below
the steep damp hill you planted with ferns,
spare and abundant in dark brown earth
above my shoulders, and across the tufts
of whitecaps above those hidden boulders;
by the back–swirling eddies the trees are full
bushes so no bank is seen here where
W.E.B. Du Bois was born after the Civil
War beside this golden–bosomed Housatonic
River, powerfully coursing through this artery,
this ventricle in the dark heart of Great Barrington.

WALDEN POND

I placed a stone atop the heap
of rubble, other rocks, with two friends
from school we walked along the shore.
Dark water, yet clear as you said, deep
right by an open sunny bank in spring.
You didn't deceive then, where a man
stood fishing. I asked him if he had
caught anything; he said, "yesterday."
Before we went around the perimeter
I saw a few languishing on a bright
slope of tender green grass, trees
bright behind them, pines and maples.
We continued around until we reached
a soft muddy cove, perch must have
swum 'neath that clear water mirror
of the sun and pale blue sky. Large
trunks lay down dying further along
a curve, strong yet giving life to other
life: insects, birds, a place for us to stop.
We took turns putting our back to wood
for a posed picture another would hold.
Atop a slope I walked along the rocks
and rails where conifers were split,
a gray heaven above, no train whistle heard.
I walked back along your shore alone.
All these years, Walden was a part
of me unseen, unknown only dreamed. This
was Early Spring in Eastern Massachusetts
under hot sun and pale sky. Then home in
the small car, past bogs, fields of lean green
marshes, grasses swaying, willows bright
as they could be, with a box full of books
that traveled across several seas.

ICARUS FLIES

Remembering now that time
when we were close and I flew
to you drawing me with your
magnetism, black magic to my
ore still unsifted but not yet
in molten state, undiminished.

Valiant with hope I flew over
a continent turning back
to you, your long soft dark
brown hair I touched at night
close as breath and lips yet
banished when we broke our kiss.

As beautiful as any on Earth
you I flew to yet could not
hold forever, your sun burning bright
melting my wings and arms,
fading from your light bright at noon
or midnight. Parting, my wings were

molten, gone. I took the train
south and home after hearing Joplin
singing, "Me and Bobby McGee." Would
I ever fly so high and close again?

A decade later we met again,
your thigh brushed and knocked
against mine. We hugged inside
that dining hall, the old place of
youth. I felt your familiar back,
curving below cropped locks.

ORPHEUS

Suffering under this burden of music,
Orpheus nearly crumbling beneath his lyre,
unsmiling in anguish on one knee, neck
stretched, head thrown back and eyes
shut he creates song silently in stone.
Rodin has his thin legs supple, no flanks
of grand Adam, but this youth out of
weakness crying to be heard or held.

No one stands in awe of his torso,
unlike Apollo or a gorgeous Eve,
but he dreams of admiration, and for
an affinity of souls. The notes rise
and fall with such passion, just as
he falters with black grandeur. He sings

for her he cannot kiss. The hours of
these summer days when only one love
may eclipse his pain. Just as the moon
is eclipsed by the Earth, then returns
full again, brightly shining like a strong
torso, that body with darker seas rising.

So, play and sing young Orpheus, the songs
of your heart strumming forlorn chords,
just as the birds sweetly warble invisible,
you rhapsodize without sound, the beauty of
that melody lasting in eternity and memory.

WASHINGTON D.C.

We walked under the same Washington
sun, three sons and a father. The stray
bum begged, "Money?" His face I remember one

afternoon: unshaven, gray–white stubble, gray
eyes like yours or mine. Ragged clothes, dirty,
draped over limbs. He foraged through that day's

collection of trash in steel wire wastebasket.
He reeked of gin, whiskey; cheeks burned red;
lids lined pink. My father gave him some bread

with barbecued chicken he cooked. We loved
the slippery white meat and sweet taste. Brothers
with a dad now single in nineteen seventy–one. Above

and below there were dry pale green and scorched tan
maple leaves lying on the ground near the pool
reflecting the sky and grass and those cherry trees full.

Now, when I remember it seems much easier to be a son
than a man. It is no easier to love the ugly than the beautiful.
We live for selfishness, or not at all when all you hold is memory.

BLACK GRANITE

We walk down in the scar, long, dark
shadowed, cool in the quiet among hushed
voices. I'd come three thousand miles for

this, unworthy as some parishioner in church,
a sinner. He had traveled nine thousand
miles from this place, his home, a mother's

son, young, long and lean. We were there
a half hour nearly before I bothered a volunteer
an older guy in vest bright in summer sun;

we couldn't find his name here in Washington.
My father told the story to me, my nieces,
nephew, me, a decade late. No, two and one

half decades late. Twenty–five years, a quarter
century and more. The span of his young life. The war
had ended, been over a day; they hadn't received

news; his helicopter crashed, shot down after
rising over the dense green brush, chopping the sky
then flames, orange, red, yellow, the black smoke.

The war ended too late for our neighbor's
son, Brian, the only one we knew never ran
in her broad and deep backyard, back to the stream

under the rustling trees in summer, water warbling
over rocks in shadows, cool, away from sun's
heat, in near–by Virginia, his mother's name too;

two Old English Sheepdogs gamboled where my brother
lived a year. We all made it home to Washington
too late. We walk up out of the earth, the dark scar

in the shadows near the quiet trees and grass, by
the obelisk and monuments beside the Potomac,
all so well planned. He not worthy of those dogs' fate.

GREEN MOUNTAIN BOY – QUETZAL

From the everyday of Michigan
to the Upper Peninsula, then to Vermont
from her to Guatemala following Muir

and Audubon, traveling so far away
a doer not just a thinker from Putney
and Marlboro, Vermont at home in

forests between the boughs of green
trees, hardwoods and conifers. O, I
can still see you a tall birch in sun

over a snow bank in your worn
blue and black Mackinaw to push "old
Bess" from snow and ice, a deep sky blue

two–door Ford Maverick to travel
down to Whitney's store, or mostly
to help a friend, true to anyone who

might benefit from your honesty.
I can still see those red tail lights
blur around the corner, and upon your

bright return pour a cold one down, joke
while throwing darts beside your slouched
seat director's chair before dinner, laughing
loud and long, taking all in your stride.

Your words, letters, deeds, your immortal
act, your "impercedero" for the resplendent
Quetzal, rare, solitary with a coughing call,
brilliant gold, emerald green and bright red.

BLACKBIRD
For S.H.

Sitting beside there then you matched
your tweed sleeve to mine, yours thatched
black and white hatched gray, mine green–
blue and black. You asked, "What are you reading?"
"Patrick Kavanagh," I said before your reciting:
"Clay is the word and clay is the flesh
where the potato–gatherers like mechanised
scarecrows move . . ." I fell silent after
"The Great Hunger." Then back to my poem
"Moss Hollow": "That gray graveled muddy
road I walked down . . . past gurgling gutter
streams of the soft shoulders." Then at
the heart you boxed in that broken line
and proffered, "The flint wing of a blackbird."

MONADNOC
for Emerson's 200th birthday

I would that we were back
at Monadnock where it's
always winter when we three
left our January mountain in
Vermont and drove down east
to New Hampshire. At the trail's
gate the deep green conifers
were heavy laden; snow drooped
boughs surrounded, a canopy
from night's fresh fall;
in the early morning silence,
just the sound of our boots
trudging through deep new–fallen
powder, wind so still within
forest below mountain as we
slowly wound up, three friends
then. We hiked, then we climbed,
winding up and past tree line
where the wind kicked up,
and the blue sky went white.
The slope was white snow, gray
ice, as our guide said, "We'll
have to cross between the cairns."
There was no trail to find.
Soon we three stooped huddled
beside granite outcropping;
wind bit fierce and he puzzled
up, squinting across for where
we might traverse to another
gray cairn, rock crop grown
from ice, bearded white. Across
cold wind bit cheeks, then below
rock face I stood left. Reaching –
"Grab my boot and pull yourself up."
Then up again atop the rock to hike
hunched across in wind, to where
we three stood atop Monadnock:

I ("glad to the brink of fear.")
We stood close and spoke below
white heaven in ice wind which
died down. "Summer you can see
clear to Boston!" But no Cambridge
or Concord seen, no birds sang
or flower found, just white snow
ice, gray rocks, snow shrouded pines
below. "In the dreaded winter time,
None save dappling shadows climb,"
he wrote, and we heard the music
of another century in wind alone
with our Monadnock before wind
kicked up and we wound down. Back
to tree line, back to forest, back
to blue sky above the trail's gate,
inexplicably watery tears flowed
from my eyes, quiet, snow blind back
below my Monadnock in deep white snow.

IN CROWS WOODS

A river bed, open dry
trees slung in humid air
deep ditch parched dry, stymied sun
banks stoop sandy brows
breeze stands still, no blind sound
birds fly between trees not looking
The black crow hacks the clouded sky.

AMERICA

Past the old brick walk
fenced in by straight iron and red
brick we saw the gentle
grass and simple lawn we
could not reach.

Here the near–by fields
were free, where we

walked the back streets
hiding our faces, and we
forgot those small marble
steps and the railing we leaned on.

OF THOSE HEROIC AND HIS SHINING SHIELD
In memory of C.K.

You spoke of those
heroic, of the Greek
epics of Homer, those
Achilles battled to seek

his glory, but quietly
we learned of his
shining shield, brightly
blinding armor this

fury wore. And the shepherd
as the spring swollen
streams rushed down
beside heard the roar.

With cool dialectic
a cryptic question seemed
akin to Socrates
in an exchange with

Plato. But like forlorn
Odysseus you were exiled
to a land formerly fat
with sheep ripe for

sacrifice. You braved
fierce and contentious
winds carving the granite
craggy to shame us

from slothful ease, to fight
through Poseidon's great
storm, that contrary tempest
raging distant from this

green slope of peace, this shore
a home for a time tempted
with immortality
but still not home.

DUCKS AT HOPKINS POND

The trees are russet, with yellow flares
and ruby red above still green water
where emerald–headed mallards
dive bill first with tail feathers in air.
Their companions speckled brown
constant beside them in autumn.

The wood's paths are cool sand or dank
black mud near trails of leaves shooshing
about my feet covered in pale brown crackling
by fallen yellow. It's been many years since bank
I sat wondering where the ducks went at winter,
or ran these trails to those blonde girls' cheers.

The girls who cheered me have long since
flown away and begun raising their young. I
have been years absent from this sky
fading towards dusk, hour before twilight,
still mirror reflecting November sky.
The pond water strewn with leaves silent.

MOUNTAIN MAN

On a winter night
of the first real snow
the windows softly glow
with the moon's lost light;

the trees are lined
with lace fine soft,
yet skeletal arms rise
to silent sky flakes fall

as I lie huddled under
covers with the cat curled
beside my soles, but with
lids shut I see your face

before my eyes, sharp
as a goldfinch's on spring
morn bright in birch,
but behind thick glasses

with dark frames, and I
see a cap pulled down with
a bill like a beak, brim
and flaps deep over ears,

like my brother's when he
shovels; then down to jowls
like an older man's, a father's
to a chin and neck a bit

droops below those thin
lips, and scratchy voice high
pitched as a pine against
the pane of Hendricks hiding

empty darkness Tom prowls
around striped and well fed.

POPPY'S WALK

On a warm Spring
day, an afternoon with
bright sun
across the brick side –
walk to the mail
box, not the nearest one.

Then we turned down
a side street,
then right again
and walked across
from the fence, above
the train tracks.
You could hear one
coming before I.

In the field we walked
all the way through;
I set you free early
on and you returned,
then again I could tell
you heard the train
and did your whirligig spins
and soon you were
racing gone along
the fence,
but you returned
smiling in sun
tongue out
unlike any lover.

So, we kept
walking all the way
down the hill
where I saw
a huge crow
bigger than a hawk
drop a squirrel,

and you pulled
hard, then under
the railroad bridge
amid broken glass,
then to another field
then along another
fence, then beside
the scraggly littered
woods, past the small
town theater
to the new soccer
fields, once a dump,
now transformed
and dedicated to a classmate's
father who I used to see
at the library and riding
his girl's bicycle.
We walked past
the girl's softball
game, the last two
outs.
     Then back across
the open soccer fields,
I tossed the tennis
ball; you ran and brought
it back, twice; you
ran down in the stony
gully between the fields.
Then we walked home.

WITH POPPY

One morning in New Hampshire,
the Green Mountains beside us
in summer at the horse farm
where we had spent the night I
walked out with the Shetland Sheep –
dog toward the huge, sloping
pasture where the thoroughbreds
grazed on the far side, there
over lush grass by the shade
of two old hardwood trees;
and they began walking over
toward us, two young chestnut
colts their coats shimmering
and one of brown, lighter in sun,
and they walked all the way
over beside the fence where
Poppy stood below me, and bowed
their long necks and heads down
that morning to pay homage to her.

SITTING BESIDE

Young boy, sitting beside on the couch
playing a game of cards called "War," you
are too young at six to truly comprehend
this. You're my nephew, little Phillip; your
mother has gone off to spend a little time
with your big brother. You smile and laugh when
you win, and I make tiny cries of woe, "Oh."

I hope you never come to this as we have,
never knowing when to say, "I love you," or
how to say "It's time to go." You hug
me so tight with all your strength before you
let go. So too with my friends, young women
always, I may never say, "I love you," before
we part company and go our separate ways.

MONTICELLO

These were his slopes
in the sun curving round
the earth like his thought
touching the wind,

framing the bricks that
remain with dome,
carefully wrought colonnade
beside the grass blades

and the dew and the birds
glide by trees here at
Monticello, its fineness
a universe in the free air.

MEETING FAITH

This First Day morning
I studied the light,
a parallelogram
divided into six panes

falling on the plain
wall in the quiet
and knew it came
from the window

in the balcony above
in this last month
ending at winter,
and I studied the light

lighting a bowed white
head of hair leaning
forward in prayer:
no easy answers here.

I couldn't see that
balcony window, but
I could see the result:
light in here from above.

FRIENDS MEETING

Those winter Sundays so long
ago, the sky so clear early light
like the quick gleam on a cufflink
before we arrived late to Meeting.

Bouncing in the old green Scout
after all the brown leaves were down
we'd park facing the fence, our backs
turned to bricks and big white wood

doors; brown knob we turned late
always, the silence broken where
one winter an old lady interrupted
a young man still speaking the sin

of bombs dropping and burning,
Napalm was replaced later by his
strumming and singing "Blowin'
in the Wind" after Meeting.

We were all tired of hearing
of the war, seeking the Divine
in silence. I was only seven.
Heaven was bouncing toward home

with my brother and dad in green
Scout to the Sunday corner store
on Potter Street for Tastykakes
after First Day School back then.

BELOW THE BUTTONWOODS
For Elizabeth Haddon

Where the grass rolls like a sea,
towering swells undulate down to peace
in this Quaker graveyard in New
Jersey, no island in a sea but an
oasis in the heart of town, a pasture
once for cows, sheep, goats,
a small wooded farm surrounded
by a wall, a lake not far beyond
the Meetinghouse there atop the slope
where we all hope to meet the Divine
on First – Day Meeting there, or
if not here amid the great trees,
huge buttonwoods like oaks,
but truly sycamores blazing white
trunks in sun here where Elizabeth rode
and strode, she who Longfellow wrote
of two centuries back in that winter
poem of here where kids still sled;
but our springs back then when the grass
was greener and the breeze was sweeter,
and we in our youth sat with each other,
one black, others white, just teens
then relaxing on viridian grass,
shades of green 'neath sun or shade
below blue sky, a spangled tapestry
of nature, and God in this place.
Boys once, but eternally human we
still seek the Divine in birds' notes
and breeze, spirit of the sun and an old
town's peace. The summer grass slopes,
rises and rolls down peopled by the stones
of Friends, some I once have known,
now just their carved names fill my
eyes with brief tears before walking on
hoping to just traipse along, descend
and rise yet again beyond the iron gate.

ABOVE A STATION OF THE BART

I rode the CalTrain north to the S.P.
Depot where I first met you who rode
that yellow and white Muni bus down

Van Ness. You wore an iridescent
silk scarf wide wrapped about your lean waist
over your faded blue jeans, your short

soft brown hair pulled straight back. Freckled
cheeks and nose shone in sun and wind as we
walked out to end of Fishermen's Wharf,

the new Pacific out beyond the wild Bay
that day. Later we sat on the grass near
Ghirardelli Square and smoked Canadian

smokes, Wisconsin and Nebraska
at your back, Massachusetts and Vermont
at mine. Nights we sat full of wine

on the basement floor of City Lights then
waiting for the bus wind kicked up and I
held you near sleep wrapped in my arms.

Months after our first date you moved north
to North Beach and I lay beside you all
night listening to you breathe, and the sea

storm wide–awake out below the moon tides.
Our last kiss was at Christmastime beside
the wooden gate of that back garden porch,

then Spring night after met by chance de–
boarding BART then riding up shining escalator;
as we rode those silver moving stairs to sky

you joked, "I'm so tall!" before smiling,
turning, then stepping into my empty arms.

WORDS OF CAPE COD

On a pad in a fine folio you
ordered I recall our conversation
of that summer, your words of your Cape Cod;
you spoke enthusiastically of that
time: "Chatham, Dennis, West Dennis,
Dennisport," and Mrs. Pickering's
Cottages; I wish now I had listened
more closely to your words, me eager
to go to the Cape, to Truro my second summer
back East; we always visited Atlantic
City as kids to see Pop Pop, but you mother,
and my dad, "Your father," you would say
had spent several summers on the Cape;
"It was your mother's idea," my father
says, but you're gone now and so is then,
that time, your time, and my first time
ten years ago. I returned many times
to Truro; this summer the first not back,
and sat atop the dune in early morning
light and watched the small birds struggle in wind
above a sand sunken fence just as I
struggle too and heard the sound of the sea
and watched the waves shoosh in and crash
then suck out, retreat quietly, and I've
noted the different gulls of white and black;
that morning I saw two porpoises swim
and glisten in gray–blue surf, but I heard you
singing in waves rolling and crashing
and in the squawks of gulls crying
to each other flying past rising sun, calling
back to one another; you were a singer too
around the house listening to the radio,
sometimes sad too; I heard more than just
celebrating–and now what can I sing?

THE OLD SCHOOL

Just outside Wigglesworth,
and below its dormered slate
roof the gray sky above us,
the summer term over with
its heat, light, sun gone,
humidity replaced by rain;
we stood beside the bricks,
the corridor tunnel before
us, you headed through, out
to Mass. Ave., me returned
over gray macadam, puddles:
"Hi, Mr. Corbett." Your
retort: "You're here!" as
you turned toward me then
awaiting the profound advice,
from teacher to student,
you said, "Get an umbrella!"

SUMMER LUSH

Just off O'Connell Street
not far from the gates of Trinity
College and St. Stephen's Green
I climbed aboard a green and tan
double–decker bus with one
purpose: to see Patrick
Kavanagh on the Grand Canal,
sitting on his park bench
there, to meet him. I spoke
up right away to the driver –
(after two days sick after cycling
a few hundred kilometers
outside of Galway I returned
by train, rested, toured Wicklow,
then barfed, then rested
again here in Dublin) –
"I want to see Patrick
Kavanagh on the Grand
Canal; can you take me
near there?" I asked, less reticent
than usual, my time winding down. "I'll
let you off near there," he
said in response to my distinct
American accent. Before long, "He's just
over there, across the street."
"Leafy – With – Love
banks and the green waters of the canal . . .";
dusk was still an hour off,
but there we met in the gloaming
below the tree shadows
the grass dark summer lush,
he bespectacled, sitting
one leg crossed over
other, jauntily lounging, smiling,
glad to see me, bespectacled,
smiling, but still lonely,
both still lonely, and later I
thought back within

to that fair young Irish
lass, blonde in café below
Laura Ashley and cobbles,
where she discussed
her studies in "Politics
at Chapel Hill," and now almost
a decade late: ("O that I were
young again and held her
in my arms!") I climbed up
above that grotto to Dublin stones
and sun that day. And later
I left Patrick Kavanagh
in the twilight and climbed
back aboard the bus far south
of the Liffey, and Inniskeen
where I've never been,
and thought back to the freckled girl
who I climbed down the bus
steps after and I walked up country road with
far west of Dublin, south of Galway with her
reciting Irish poetry after exams were over.

WILD SUMMER SWANS AT COOLE

The grass was tender green, the banks dank;
the water brimming and rippling white sun
as I stood beside the bank in sinking
earth unable to go further. I could only go back.
Across the water blinding and sparkling those
small white summer swans, brilliant
birds in flight nearly beyond my sight.

I sat on a stone among the stones
scratched with kids' initials,
their graffiti of love unending.
No longer a kid, and my ancestors
long gone from this island, and those
islands lit in sun. Only in memory
is love alive, white birds, white swans.

TO THOOR BALLYLEE

I hired a hack or cab
or taxi from Gort? After
by a day at least Coole
Park where I walked up
'neath those leaning trees
and through the great canopy,
and winding over sandy trails
to Lough in sun, rocks
by beach, white birds
far off . . . but to Thoor
Ballylee I rode up hilly
winding country road
slowing for some sheep,
with an Irish driver happy
to accommodate me:
"Take your time, all
the time you need." Up those
winding stairs I wound
in Yeats's Norman Tower,
home for George Hyde Lees,
but far above I peered down
through fortress windows cut
in stone to deep lush thick green
pasture between the trees
in air above where sheep
did graze . . . Thoor Ballylee
Thoor Ballylee home to Yeats
and George Hyde Lees carved
in stone too below, and did
his specter linger here
up that winding stair climbing
up to room in air, here
where he lived above, winding
in his gyre like a falcon
circling in sky oft pale
blue, or gray with rain

falling over lush summer green
grass as thick as maiden's hair:
"Does the imagination dwell the most
Upon a woman won or lost?"

AT THE BOATHOUSE
   For Dylan and Caitlin Thomas

I stood there looking out
    across the blazing
        blue Taf estuary
To Sir John's verdant
    hill across
        the bright
           light
blue and white water
    glittering
        from
    tufts of clouds
        on this
late afternoon in Laugharne.
I stood beside your workshed
    painted blue with drafts
        of poems still strewn
           on the floor,
              an empty
    brown bottle, a print tacked
        to the wall beside
        a photo of
                    Auden.
But I didn't hear you bellowing,
    just the cormorants crying
        in the sun.
Walking further up the path
    shadowed by the towering
        trees I arrived
        to your
            boathouse
        and went inside standing before
        the mantle with two white
            china Staffordshire
                dogs just like those
                  we had at home.

I looked out the small windows
    to the gleaming water,
        then studied a small, framed
photograph of you Dylan: "Son of the Wave"
    in Welsh with your wife
Caitlin, Irish beside:
    you two I came to see.

THROUGH THE GARDEN
In memory of R.M.J.

You are present with those bounding brows,
sidelong glances, brown eyes squinting, smiling.
I filled notebooks with class notes, but you
never needed any, just glancing down
to the book in question, or looking out
clear glass panes of Dalrymple, the white
clapboard converted barn with your character
and your integrity evident on your visage.
Whether "The Puritans" or "The Transcendentalists"
edited by Perry Miller, or Emerson or Thoreau
or Cooper and "Natty Bumppo" or William
James, you knew them all. I became "Dan'l"
before we embarked on "The History
of the American Frontier" or "Henry David
Picker" as I read back from E.B. White
into H.D. Thoreau, and his essay "Walking."
... No, you are forever present, glasses
pushed up above brows, or wrapped by string,
or in those cups of tea, or dog walks bounding.
Or, after lunch and tea I recall, that last
walk through the garden door, over lawn,
then down the road, not Bjorn or Crispin
but Cooper beside, after you signed
your book with fountain pen back inside,
then stride we did down the hill, Cooper
with you content – ("Splendid" you would
say on the bleakest winter day) – then
after we shook hands that last time,
and before you turned back up the slope
you broke into song and sang melodious
as a cheerful bird; I wish I asked what
tune it was, just following the lilting
song but not all of your kind words.

BRIDGES

You're my safe bridge
over the churning grim
gray Delaware, the paved
road clear and lit at night,
the city lights stars sparkling.

You're my Bay Bridge
dark trestles, the top deck
open after leaving Berkeley
driving south past the city
toward the peninsula dark
hour past midnight then home.

You're my Golden Gate:
the most beautiful bridge
on Earth stretching from
the Marin foothills above
Sausalito to the Presidio
back to the city by the bay,

on a bright day the water
far below blue blinding bright
the sailboats sleek white
jostling, contend with
spinnakers full billowing,
taut lines stretched.

You're my wooden bridge
in an old forest familiar
as home with a nymph
cavorting and the night
birds' "shhhh," just the moon
on the pond with willows.

FOR LOVE OF THE MODERN

That white blossom with white
heart, stamen and pistil
by pure white petals
soft and open by white leaves
touched by faint green:
O'Keeffe
of light and shadow but mostly light,
Stieglitz admired
those petals: "White Calico Flower"
1931 by Georgia O'Keeffe.

"The Figure 5 in Gold"
Explodes from red
And orange
And black and gray
And white
near C.D. in red
and W.C.W.
under the bottom
curving large
Number 5,
above Bill
in Chinese Red
near Carlo . . . faint in
orange
obscured
floating.

On another
wall a yellow
flower with
big brown
heart
blooms above
two red
ripened fruit
of Charles Demuth
"From the Kitchen Garden":

a tomato an apple a pepper
beside a deep purple eggplant – in 1925.

"PARKER'S BACK"
   For Flannery O'Connor

His back, body, skin stained
His flesh works, the deed done
His soul in dark ink dripped from needle piercing
His person, a son, a groom once, a husband
His will endures the kneeling, crouching below

Her gaze downward, disdaining under sun or moon
    trees' boughs and stars over loam
    wet with dew languishing diadems.

Her bones bend, fingers raw to touch
    worked in water of home
    of kitchen, of dishes and plates
    by a window where branches reach
       and the bird flits singing beneath
       her look to that feathered
       iridescence that provokes no
       wonder, those cries that rise
       to near deaf ears, those rising
       swirls of color dripping like blood
       from a crown converging
         over

His back of flesh, skin over sinews, tendons bent
    in adoration, bowing below to show
    the ornate pattern a paradigm
    of the eternal above dust
    snakes inhale, scaly creatures crawling
    through dusk light failing, the whole creation
    leaning below
    her hard eyes not seeing,
       her ears not hearing the whole creation crying
         mercy –

AMISTAD'S DREAM

Those dark beams creak
as low voices groan,
locked below in hold
as the hull lists in wind

still, the plash of waves
and tide shift as planks
are buffeted by sea swells
rising so far from home,

then the clank of iron
over planks, the heavy drag
of chains locked to ankles,
wrists ripped, dragged from

the amber bosom of
mother Africa, Sierra
Leone of tan sand,
the viridian forests

inland, to be sold far from
where monkeys cavort in
jungle breeze playing
free near the iridescent

birds red–feathered
and yellow gold, fluttering
to soar over bright stripes
of those free creatures.

AT EIGHT

Lying on my stomach looking down, the big white
pad before my elbows, endlessly drawing on the unlined
side in pen, or magic marker. Clean sheets a gift
from dad, and RCA. Or sitting atop the radiator
in the living room watching the early morning sky
as my father is outside near the open cellar door
and mother is above him in the kitchen in June
and he listens to the radio not far from his cans
of screws and nails neatly sorted in the shadowed
dust, or lifts a sledge hammer before the news
comes on: Robert Kennedy was shot and killed
last night in Los Angeles. And he drops the steel
mallet on his foot and cries. It is nineteen sixty–eight
and I am not yet nine as I watch the robins.

OUR LAST HIKE

Our last hike through the Pennsylvania woods
we sat by the spring washing our feet
and necks and heads and laughed.

Ned, in the morning we looked down
the same slope to the sun
and dreamed of our journey going on

every step of sweat in the noon sun
over those boulders where we grew.

LAST LATE NIGHT SONG

The last night is not gone
But caught in the light wind
Coolness and midnight sound
Of crickets and cicadas.

Down the slow–curving hill
Is the field in night stillness
With the old giant weeping
Willow half felled
And the thick coarse grass wet
And hard under bare soles.

You reach the coarse yellow
Grass under the morning star.

The trees reach to the sun
And thin limbs leaves blown
By breeze let the white light
Shine through.

Here the water no longer gleams
And in the dead river bed
The woods stretch to the sound
Of the far rolling route
That the birds sing over
And the hawk glides past.

Between the tall tight
Trees sing of the lost
Woods that won't die.

FIELD BY THE CORN

That fall when we lay
in that field by the corn,
by the wide river, in
the dew I watched the stars

fall down the dark sky,
those distinct hard points
as I touched you, and couldn't
wish to touch too much.

FAMINE VESSEL

I could only dream
standing below the deck
what they dreamed in
the shadowed dark, half

lit. I could only dream
in those cozy bunks
blankets beside the boards
sound as the hull crashed

and cut through gray
and black stormy north
Atlantic sea, an ocean
crossed and re-crossed:

those crossings became
her cross as mast
rose in air and cloth
billowed and stretched

beside spar, and strung
sails filled with invisible
wind pushed and pulled
them all safe across.

I could only dream
with hand wrapped
round taut rope of her
crossing from island home

of that famine–stricken
isle of the starving
Irish, of my great–
grandmother above in sun

light bright noon
above the mast sky
clear blue and spray
splashing as her bow cut

through, from old home
to new home, from land
of no hope, craggy,
to land of all hope alone.

O, I can only dream
your dreams Jeanie
Johnston below deck
in half–lit dark,

or above in noon
sun. The only ship
that never knew death
with flag of green flying,

and sails billowing,
cold water spraying
hull's boards holding
the mother safely home.

FOR MY FATHER

Where would I meet you, after you had gone,
I am a small man, you a small man. At
thirteen you told me I was a man, and years
before that you re–iterated Abraham's
legacy, tradition. You used to sit before
the back shed door opening up to a porch
and world beyond, thick forest of maples
cherry trees, wild, the tulip poplar
housed blue–jays, cardinals, robins
diving after blossoms near those
cream peach colored flowers at Spring.

There was the orange clay we shoveled
by the new rooms, you cursed the builders,
you a mason; are not we too just clay in
wind and rain. That yard became my world
after you had gone, daffodils and crocuses
too precious to pluck for mother. The dogs,
the snakes, cats, rabbits, chipmunks at home
there. After homemade cherry pies I found
all your old papers in the basement, bright
colors of *The New Frontier* all those
kids smiling. By the sea we had swum
in sun and salt breeze where you grew
with your father too. Or camping across
the country, those dreams were dreams
for me, from the Pacific to the Potomac
where Washington threw a coin, a gamble
below the same sky now near towers
glistening white by domes.
                You hollered when
you found I had cut–up all you saved,
and took the cabinets away. I was left with
pictures, the calendar of him behind your head
with a crimson background, the short hair
by the turquoise stove near where you listened

to the news, cried and hurt yourself.
I was left with the local ponds and lakes
sun mud and snails.

GULLS

I remember the pink china gulls
high up over the stove that held
the huge pot of chicken soup simmering
in that immaculate, organized, white

kosher kitchen where diminutive Nanny
hovered. From Vienna, her maiden
name Vogel means bird in German.
Pop–pop near with his booming

voice, his son, my Pop, my father
and the soup Pop–pop's specialty
as we waited patiently, quietly
five grandkids, mom, with hunger.

Outside the awnings flapped brightly
in the shore summer breeze beyond
the enameled railings, the porch balcony
blue and white, Harry's three–storey

"Cottage," the American Dream with
old glory fluttering near the lighthouse.
They're both gone now, he nearly
a decade when I last saw him in

the front room, screened in sun porch
of a quieter neighborhood three blocks
from the beach. We shook hands on
Father's Day, and he gave me that strong

grasp of silent recognition smiling;
Pop–pop I should've visited more often
but still the white gulls dance in sunlight
intense like youth's pleasures, brief, unlike

family. These gulls spin, swoop like Spitfires.

THE CANDLE BURNS
In memory of D.G.

The candle burns on the high hutch
varnished deep brown wood, wide grain holds
the finest china for special occasions, the high

holidays when we would sit quietly, heads
bowed, elbows held in, the Seder herb
bitter herb, is not this too much to bear?

Eyes closed, chins dropped in prayer,
solemn we hope for the best, the best
taken from us, President of A.Z.A.

under B'nai B'rith, President;
is it not too much to remember
the flame, the warm wax, liquid

clear like tears. Or, on the small
bookcase near the kitchen table the gold
plaques rest, or hung above. The candle

burns, the flame lives beside blue
ribbons for excellence, accomplishment,
the best called for, taken from us.
Quiet in prayer lost a brother, son.

Now I remember our tennis match,
my first, so long ago; that old wooden racket
once held by press, I swung, and those
shots he hit so hard and well, returned.

CLOTHESPIN
   In memory of Moni

    "I am for an art that tells you the time of day,
or where such and such a street is. I am for an art
that helps old ladies across the street." – Claes

Not one of mom's weathered
wooden clothespins in the hard woven
basket in the back shed for the line
which runs from above the back
deck high up clear across the back
yard to the huge double tulip poplar
gone now, she and you, too, but Claes's sculpture
set back on 15th Street: "Meet me at
'The Clothespin'!" you'd say, then joke: "I'll need
a clothespin to hold my nose!" I knew it
in Center City near City Hall, then
when I would see you standing there in
sun, your brown hair lit above smile,
I felt the thrill like wind within
from having a friend. "Less is more," Mies
said, but I am more akin to Browning,
my mother's favorite; I cannot cut
this short like your soft brown hair.
We'd explore Sansom Street: Taylor's Country
Store, a bit of Vermont gone now too
from this City of Brotherly Love, this
Philadelphia, or Joseph Fox Books
downstairs then. I took you to Smedley's
a block up from Joe's where I met you
too. But it was the AIA Bookstore
you introduced me to too, clean, neat,
organized, beautiful architecture
books closest to who you were, where you came
from, then there was back to Vermont, Brattle–
boro and up the mountain, but "What does
a mountain care?" You're gone. You were never
my Lucrezia, though I wished you
were. "Well, less is more, Lucrezia: . . ."

I was a painter once too, before then.
You are in heaven now. "Ah, but a man's
reach should exceed his grasp, or what's a heaven
for?" mother tried to teach me. But up
the mountain I held your shoulders in my
hands those nights, then next, another season,
back to Olde City in summer grass green
and sloping near Carpenter's Hall, 18th
century beauty we close side–by–side
reclined, then years later first deep kiss
below grove of eucalyptus trees in
Palo Alto, then back in San Francisco
late by past midnight fire soft wet kisses,
full warm you at winter on cool fresh
white sheets . . . – then Spring, the Getty in
Malibu, our villa, our dream of
Roman order atop cliff in bright sun;
"Mali–boo–boo" you called it after you
stumbled crossing the street, the Coast Highway, –
or the Huntington Garden south; further
back I travel in memory, out of
order, – the steps through wood down to gray
Bay Bridge water, ships slowly sailing away
to some other world. Up the Sir Francis
Drake we drove one morning after in
that white, top–down Love Bug; – I had been
a kind sir back in Vermont, but I wish
I could mutter as Andrea spoke:
"I regret little, I would change still less." . . .
"This must suffice me here. What would one have?
In heaven, perhaps, new chances, one more chance"?
So much gone you old friend so young then
too young to leave this earth, so much never ends.

THOSE DAYS IN SUN

Then in summer I would call
and ride my bike across town
to meet you at "the club" to
which you rode your bike too,
in tennis shorts and shirt, no
t–shirts then; I then with
my Dunlop Maxply Fort near
the same as yours, 4 and 5/8
a bit big for my small hand,
but just the same as yours.

We'd hit and rally before
dusk when most everyone
was gone, sliding on the old
red clay those summer days
when it didn't rain. You
the taller stronger blonder
hit with heavy topspin I
could hardly handle, a shorn
Bjorn Borg who smiled.
After everyone was gone we

would hit across three courts,
lobbing high and out of sight
in the gloaming; then you'd
swat a ball beyond the fence
trying to hit the dark–windowed
brick apartment buildings across
the cavernous train tracks. All
that's still there, but you
are gone, my old friend I hadn't
seen in decades. There was one

spring match, though I didn't win
and rarely beat you was worth all
the losses; I saw well enough in sun
that day as we rallied endlessly,
both showing off for the girl
on the next court who hit
with the older basketball star;
she with long blonde hair I
sat next to in Physics class
sharing my faceless drawings,

both smiling; but she with her taller
partner that day in last century's
sun rallied but not as well as us
as we slid perfectly into every
shot striking just inside the lines;
they paused awed and watched us,
she the teenage babe who said
in school days later, "You're good."

SOCCER: CENTENNIAL FIELD

When we were all part of that team,
you the smiling warrior witty beside
the sideline, after the battle, the practice,

the proving was over, we were all left
united by sweat glowing gleaming,
grass stained, satisfied, smiling, pleased,

relieved it was over in the autumn,
the fall evening now dark cool under
lights just a wrapped–up soccer practice;

I remember well you the elder: Varsity
across field grass, skilled, tenacious. So
it's all past now below the slope,

the dark green field free of our
trampling cleats, abandoned by me,
one of the mere freshmen. Then later

you became the Harvard man, two
degrees, "a sharpie" a friend
of mine then said in complimentary jest.

You left behind a wife, four sons, one
about to commence from your alma mater,
my school too, but I of no glory

to live on, except in my memory
beside the sideline, the field, the battle
practice done, there sweaty, just equals.

That one practice when I played
well, I at halfback, the midfielder
stepping right with our coach, we meshed

as a perfect team to combat the starters
at Varsity under those early stars
just assembling above, gods watching,

that one late evening battle practice
all our passing moving over field grass,
cleats pivoting, feet kicking, at Centennial.

RED TAIL HAWK

You, there, elegant cream and tan
feathered fury so close, down on
this ground, yellow beak, eyes
intent, fixed with black circles zeroed
in on your prey caught in talons
on the soft damp ground still dank
winter weeks before spring; there
I see you so fiercely pull,
shred, peck another bird helpless
fresh, dead. You, an Iliadic
raptor who soars above our
counties, as "Zeus sees the wide
world," Red – Tailed Hawk home
here with muted deep red tail
feathers the color of dried blood.
Hawk, I've never seen you so
close; I need not peer through
upper reaches of my windshield –
you worthy of glinting shield –
light breaking through those
wings outstretched in wind,
far up friend or foe circling, near
hovering, eyeing me forlorn
wishing for half your grandeur,
half your power to descend,
plummet, snatch, then ascend again.
Your fire near silent elegant as wind.

HEADED HOME

He was the only older man other than
my father who I ever threw a baseball
with before our house. I could tell his
body was old, as he bent down often
a little bit slow. A handful of years
later he came to live with us. Tears
were in my eyes. Now I hold those
years like fine gravel in my hands, and let
the wind take it away, when I hear
the distant cries, and voices of people
yelling and happy, as a man rounds third.

The last time I saw him he was laid out
and hollow, with a gray–white hue. I
was afraid to hover too long by those
flowers, yellow, red, before I kneeled down
to pray. Our dear Lord took him home as
he will to all someday. I studied the beads
'round his then still earthy hands. His
strong body was diminished, and the light
in his eyes was gone. That late afternoon
after the Mass by the priest who knew him
from loved one's voices best, I stood
below the huge full–leaved oaks rustling
in the deep blue summer sky, on green grass.

STEEP STONY ROAD

I walked down the road we had walked,
two sons and our mother that summer
afternoon in August in Vermont. Talked
we did of the rocky gravel: "It's tough
going over these rocks," you said as stones
shifted under foot below the trees rustling
in wind, you in white pumps and long sky
blue dress. Mom, I thought it would be good
for you, us, to walk to the Homer Noble
farm, then up to Frost's cabin in woods by
field; (I recalled it much closer from years
before.) But it was hard on sixty–three–
year–old legs. You rested with a son
on a boulder an ice–age glacier left,
by the white clapboard farmhouse before we
walked further up the gravel path to the cabin.
(I'd no idea then you had only six years left.)
I'd been away out west and memory
held you in Uncle's old saying: "She could
run like a deer!" You had not been back
to Vermont for a decade, and many more
since you worked the dairy farm near: milking
cows at dawn, pitching hay bales at noon,
calling cows before dusk, earning the same
wages as the men. Now years too late I
say, "I'm sorry mom for asking you to walk
all the way up the steep stony road to Frost's
cabin," but it's too late for words. I have
returned here with you and without. So
maybe now this walk will help me as
I bound down below trees blown by brisk wind
and the fall maples begin to turn red
as the air breathes over green grass leaves.

STEEP STONY ROAD by Daniel Picker includes
his poem "River Goddess":
WINNER of The Dudley Review Poetry Prize from
HARVARD UNIVERSITY for 2010.
In selecting the Prize – Winning poem
"River Goddess" the Judge wrote:

"This poem compelled me from the outset, with an opening line that bravely reclaims the river image that governs T.S. Eliot's majestic third quartet. The question in my mind was: *Can the author sustain such a bold gesture and make it something more than a postmodern gimmick?* Patiently and sinuously moving from timelessness to time, from the pastoral to the industrial, the author does indeed succeed by guiding the reader in a Frostian 'directive' through to the final four lines in which, as at the bottom of a great river (in this case, the Housatonic), we arrive at the turbulent agent of the poem: the stirrer of social change and articulate observer of the aftermath of Reconstruction, W.E.B. DuBois. In a mere 16 lines, the author achieves a remarkably subtle and yet potent poem of historical reawakening and literary resonance."
– Christina Davis, Curator of the Woodberry Poetry Room,
Harvard University

I would like to thank Harvard University, Dudley House,
The Dudley Review, and all those affiliated with *The Dudley Review* of 2010.

Special thanks are due to TS of Viral Cat Press.

ABOUT THE AUTHOR:

Daniel Picker's poem "River Goddess" was chosen as Winner of The Dudley Review Poetry Prize from Harvard University for 2010. "River Goddess" was selected by Christina Davis, Curator of The Woodberry Poetry Room at Harvard University. Daniel Picker has received a Fellowship from the Geraldine R. Dodge Foundation and The Fine Arts Work Center. Daniel Picker grew up in Haddonfield, New Jersey and graduated from Haddonfield Memorial High School. He studied at The Pennsylvania Academy of the Fine Arts, and then Marlboro College in Marlboro, Vermont where he earned a B.A. in American Studies. Daniel Picker studied English in the Graduate School of Arts & Sciences at Harvard University. He then studied English literature in Lincoln College, Oxford, and earned an M.A. in English from Middlebury College in Middlebury, Vermont. Daniel Picker has worked as a Writer and Editor for Stanford University in the Asia Pacific Research Center and as a Journalist and Sportswriter for several publications.

The poems, reviews, a memoir, articles, and short prose works by Daniel Picker have appeared in *Harvard Review*, *The Oxonian Review*, *The Philadelphia Inquirer*, *Middlebury Magazine*, *Rain Taxi Review of Books*, *The Dudley Review* at Harvard, *Elysian Fields Quarterly: The National Baseball Journal*, *Poetry* (Chicago), *Dial Tone: Stanford's Journal of the Arts*, *Sequoia: The Stanford Literary Magazine*, *Soundings East*, *RUNE: MIT Journal of Arts & Letters*, *The Princeton Packet*, *The Stanford Daily*, *The Country Almanac*, *The Haddon Herald*, *ShampooPoetry*, *Folio*, *I'll Watch Anything*, *Vermont Literary Review*, *Art Calendar Magazine*, and many others.

www.ingramcontent.com/pod-product-compliance
Lightning Source LLC
Chambersburg PA
CBHW031205090426
42736CB00009B/793